OUTRAGEOUS
OFFICE
DARES

SUZIE
DUNCAN

OUTRAGEOUS OFFICE DARES

Summersdale Publishers Ltd
46 West Street
Chichester
West Sussex
PO19 1RP
UK

www.summersdale.com

Printed and bound in Great Britain

ISBN: 978-1-84024-775-6

Substantial discounts on bulk quantities of Summersdale books are available to corporations, professional associations and other organisations. For details telephone Summersdale Publishers on (+44-1243-771107), fax (+44-1243-786300) or email (nicky@summersdale.com).

CONTENTS

INTRODUCTION

The majority of us spend forty hours a week slaving away at a miserable job we do not like, to reach meaningless targets we do not care about, for a soul-sapping boss we have little respect for. But, hurrah – all is not lost. Many of us share the misery of the daily grind and thankfully there is something that can be done.

Do you feel the urge to spice things up a little? Are you are a non-conformist with a devilish sense of humour?

Now is the time to embrace your inner delinquent. All that is required is this book (small enough to be hidden in any desk drawer), a strong head and an open mind.

Remember: we are all in this together and it is up to each and every one of us to make the workplace a little more tolerable.

WARNING: Playing Outrageous Office Dares will not reward you with the promotion you have always dreamed of, but rest assured you will leave the office safe in the knowledge that you have brightened up the day of every employee. Or just confused the hell out of them.

A QUICK NOTE ABOUT THE POINT SYSTEM

The dares have been given a carefully graded point system. Warm yourself up with the one point dares: they are perfect for the confident beginner or for your first day with a new company.

The three point dares are relatively easy to perform but are often so subtle they may go unnoticed.

The five point dares are not to be taken lightly. They are challenging and somewhat outrageous. Expect very puzzled glances and to lose friends.

Turn straight to the ten point dares if your contract is coming to an end or if you sense your P45 is looming on the horizon.

Play the game, if you dare...

1 POINT DARES

Whenever you speak, hold your hairbrush to your mouth like it's a microphone.

Spend the entire day on Facebook and insist that you're 'networking'.

Swap the sugar for salt then complain to your boss.

Snort and roll your eyes just before anyone speaks to you.

START HAVING CONVERSATIONS WITH THE PHOTOCOPIER.

STEAL YOUR BOSS'S MUG AND HOLD IT TO RANSOM.

Decide which film stars your colleagues best resemble and call everyone by their film star name for the whole day.

stop using punctuation and capital letters

Switch the lights on and off twenty times in succession.

Announce to the office that you caught your other half wearing your underwear. Ask, 'Is this normal?'

When talking to a colleague, waffle and trail off your sentences, look distant then suddenly say, 'So it's a date!'

Talk like Bart Simpson for a whole day.

Tippex a Polo mint and put it back in the packet. Offer them around and see who gets the altered one.

Start the day with ten star jumps in front of your desk.

Give your male colleagues fishnet stockings and tell them you've just seen *Chicago* and feel inspired to have a themed day.

Scratch your back against the walls and office dividers at regular intervals during the day, moaning with pleasure as you do so.

Invite everyone in the office to a naturist party you're throwing at the weekend.

Burp the alphabet.

Consume sachets of ketchup in front of your colleagues and announce that it's the latest fad diet.

Tell the new office starter that every Tuesday is 'dress-down day'.

Wear vampire fangs and say, 'I'm going to suck... [long pause] your blood!'

Hide all the milk.

Read a poem or hymn at the start of the day.

Stare at someone across the desk, pretending to nod off when they notice you.

Ask the office assistant whether it's possible to send your emails by first rather than second class, since you need to make sure they arrive the next day.

When someone offers you a cup of tea, say you'd prefer a cup of beer.

Cackle maniacally and rub your hands together every time you receive an email.

Bring a large collection of Beanie Babies to work and arrange them artistically around your desk.

Insist that everyone remove their shoes (and socks for an extra point) before entering the meeting room.

Hum quietly through your nose while looking unassuming and keeping a straight face.

STRIKE TWO KEYS ALTERNATELY FOR FIFTEEN MINUTES WHILST STARING INTENTLY AT THE SCREEN.

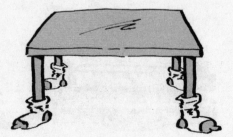

SEND A DOCUMENT WITH THE WORDS 'HELP ME I'M STUCK IN THE PRINTER, GET ME OUT!!!!!!' TO YOUR BOSS'S PRINTER.

FINISH ALL EMAILS WITH THE WORD 'INNIT' FOR A DAY.

Pretend you're a human beatbox for five minutes.

Precede every stroke of the 'backspace' or 'delete' key by saying out loud 'Oops, that wasn't meant to happen!'

Move your monitor and keyboard as far apart as their cables will allow. Begin working.

Wander about the office sharpening your pencils. When you have finished sharpening yours, offer to sharpen everyone else's.

Call your boss 'squire' for the day.

Earnestly ask your boss if there is a company drill in the event of a nuclear attack.

Wear a cape rather than a jacket to work and 'swoosh' around corners.

Join your eyebrows together using a permanent marker. Draw a curly moustache for two extra points.

PRECEDE EVERY SENTENCE YOU SPEAK WITH 'NO OFFENCE BUT...'.

DEVELOP AN ANNOYING NERVOUS TIC WHENEVER SOMEONE TRIES TO HOLD A CONVERSATION WITH YOU.

Try to convert your workmates to Scientology.

Ask everyone what their favourite apple variety is. When they look puzzled, offer to go first and say, 'I like Cox.'

Put green food colouring in the milk.

Try to include a pun in every sentence for the whole day.

Threaten to leave your job if your simplest requests are not met. For instance, 'I'll resign if you don't put two sugars in my tea,' or 'Pass me the stapler or I'll quit.'

Sing songs from musicals – try to convince others to join in.

Burst into tears at the end of the day, claiming that you 'don't want to go home'.

Spill a glass of milk on the floor and cry over it.

Refuse to speak to any of your colleagues unless they address you as 'Monsignor'.

Hum the first seven notes of an eight-note scale and wait to see if anyone feels compelled to complete it.

Hold swivel chair races – first to fifty spins wins.

Mumble incoherently to a colleague and then say, 'I hope you got that, I don't want to have to repeat myself.'

Vacuum around your desk – for half an hour.

Keep a fork on your desk so that when your boss asks you to do something, you can look at them through the prongs and imagine them in jail.

Swap round the cables to your colleagues' computer monitors.

Create a photo collage of your 'pets' – the more obscure the better, e.g. a blue whale, a condor, a greater bilby.

DEMAND YOUR COLLEAGUES ADDRESS YOU BY YOUR
WRESTLING NAME, 'ICE MAN'.

WHEN SITTING IN A MEETING, SLOWLY EDGE YOUR
CHAIR TOWARDS THE DOOR.

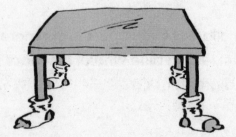

Perform yoga at your desk for an hour at lunchtime. (Extra point for wearing Lycra).

Bring a framed photograph of the Royal Family to work and mount it on the wall. Tell people it inspires you.

After every sentence, say 'mon' in a bad Jamaican accent e.g. 'The files are on your desk, mon.'

While giving a presentation leave your flies open for one hour. If anyone points it out, reply, 'I know. I prefer it this way.'

Read aloud your favourite children's story during quiet periods.

On arrival at your desk, plead with your computer that you don't want to fight today and that you are doing your best.

Set the start-up tone of a colleague's computer to a sheep baaing.

Email the whole department frequently with trivial information e.g. 'My office will be closed at 3.42 p.m. for six minutes while I shred some documents.' Apologise for the inconvenience.

1 POINT DARES

While you are waiting for documents to print, stand on your head and sing 'Is This the Way to Amarillo'.

Drop your chair as low as it will go. Complain loudly that your desk is too high.

Wear rubber gloves whenever you use your computer. If your antics are questioned, simply mutter, 'Infections... everywhere' repeatedly to yourself.

Set the screensaver of a colleague's PC to a slideshow of unlikely heart-throbs e.g. David Hasselhoff, Chesney Hawkes, Pat Sharp...

Switch keyboards with a colleague without their knowledge. Type messages on the screen for them. (Extra point if they tell you God is talking to them through their computer.)

Hang a two foot-long piece of toilet roll from the back of your pants. Act genuinely surprised when someone points it out.

When using the lift, each time the doors close and it starts its trip to the next floor, hum the *Mission Impossible* theme tune.

Wear an abundance of bling. Refer to colleagues as 'homeys'.

EAT A LOT OF GARLIC FOR LUNCH FOR A WEEK. BE SURE TO BREATHE ON COLLEAGUES.

MAKE YOURSELF A HANDY OFFICE UTILITY BELT AND FILL IT WITH STATIONERY. CHARGE PEOPLE FOR THE HIRE OF ITS CONTENTS.

PIMP YOUR OFFICE CHAIR USING SEQUINS AND LIGHTS.

Create an obstacle course for your colleagues to navigate on their way to the photocopier. Chairs and filing cabinets make excellent barricades, while the shredder adds a little frisson of danger.

Wear only pink clothes for a day.

Before starting work on a Monday morning, stand on a chair, ring an imaginary bell and shout in your deepest voice, 'Let's Get Ready to Ruuumble' in the style of a boxing announcer.

Eat five doughnuts at lunch without licking your lips. If someone points out the sugar on your face, tell them it's your beard.

Make yourself a set of dentures using Blu-Tack.

Discreetly lean over and sniff a colleague's armpit.

Invent a fictional television series and quote its 'hilarious' catchphrases during every conversation e.g. 'What's that in your hair, biggun?' Express disbelief when your colleagues say they don't know what you're talking about.

Address a casual meeting as a 'symposium' and address the attendees as 'delegates'.

WHEN WALKING TO AND FROM YOUR DESK, SING
'LEFT FOOT, RIGHT FOOT, LEFT FOOT,
RIGHT FOOT...'.

SPEAK ABOUT YOURSELF IN THE THIRD PERSON
FOR A DAY.

WHILST A COLLEAGUE IS AWAY FROM THEIR COMPUTER, TAKE A SCREENSHOT OF THEIR DESKTOP AND SAVE IT AS THEIR WALLPAPER, DELETE ALL THEIR ICONS FROM THE DESKTOP, THEN AWAIT THEIR FUTILE CLICKING...

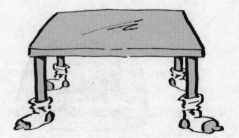

Whistle the theme tune from *The Great Escape* and place a muddy tablespoon prominently on your desk.

Insist each conversation, no matter how trivial, ends in a high five.

Claim to have learnt to do backflips, then walk backwards through the office. Act surprised when everyone says they didn't see it and mutter something about being too fast to be seen by the human eye.

Make up nicknames for all your colleagues and refer to them only by these names all day: 'No, I'm sorry, I'm going to have to disagree with you there, Chachi.'

Try to include poetic techniques in your speech and emails, such as rhyme, alliteration and onomatopoeia.

Offer to make your colleagues tea or coffee and serve it without water or milk.

Offer palm readings to your colleagues. When the office coward accepts, stare at their palm for a while then back away, trembling.

Claim to have a horrible body deformity, but don't let any of your colleagues see it.

PASTE PICTURES OF SHEEP AROUND
THE OFFICE AND TELL EVERYONE THAT
IT'S JUST YOUR LITTLE HOBBY.

CARRY A BAG OF PEBBLES EVERYWHERE WITH YOU. IF ANYONE ASKS, TELL THEM THEY'RE MAGIC PEBBLES AND YOU 'NEED THEM FOR PROTECTION FROM THE MICROWAVE RADIATION ALL AROUND US'.

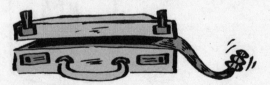

3 POINT DARES

Wear water skis at your desk and tell everyone you're practising for a tropical holiday.

When asked a question, pause thoughtfully for a moment. Then answer with a reply that rhymes with the question. For example, in reply to 'Where's the stapler?' you say, 'By the paper.' Do this all morning and see if anyone notices.

When asked to take minutes in a meeting, jump up, run and yell, 'No time! No time!'

Spread a rumour about yourself, then complain to HR.

RANDOMLY SING ALONG TO CHEESY 80S MUSIC EVERY DAY AT NOON.

LAUGH ECSTATICALLY AND DECLARE TO THE ENTIRE OFFICE THAT YOU DON'T EVEN KNOW HOW YOU GOT THIS JOB CONSIDERING EVERYTHING ON YOUR CV IS A COMPLETE LIE.

Psychoanalyse everyone's behaviour and talk in an Austrian accent all day long.

Change the time on the office clocks regularly.

Wrap everything on your desk in tin foil or newspaper.

In the 'subject heading' of all emails write, 'For sexual favours' or 'In memory of...'

Every phone call you make, pretend that the person you are ringing has just rung you. Repeat until you hear the line go dead.

Pretend to make a hushed phone call to someone called John, and tell them you can't stop thinking about them.

Arrive at work in your dressing gown, holding a bowl of cornflakes.

Throw a 'new stationery' party every time the delivery man from the stationery supplier arrives.

Create walls with files and boxes and if anyone tries talking to you, tell them to respect your walls.

Spend the morning trying to scratch your armpit with your big toe.

Go up to a random colleague and demand to know why they stood you up last night.

Say 'in bed' at the end of every sentence.

Wear a beret, bright red lipstick and dark sunglasses at your desk. If anyone bothers you, shrug your shoulders and say *'Je ne sais quoi.'*

Start yapping like an excited puppy.

Bring in a baseball bat and point to the pigeons on the roof, muttering that 'they're gonna get it'.

Introduce your imaginary friend Womsoll to the new office starter.

Offer to file some of your co-worker's papers, throw them up in the air and yell, 'Hooray, confetti!'

Wear flippers for shoes.

Come to work with your leg in a cast, holding crutches. Swing the crutches at your colleagues and tell them you'll get them back.

Sniff some pepper at the staff meeting.

As everyone leaves the meeting room, stand by the door and offer them a stick of rock. Hit them with it if they refuse.

Erect an enormous sign above your desk emblazoned with the words 'Do Not Disturb' written in a selection of felt tips and glitter pens.

Pick up a phone and have a conversation with yourself. When someone asks, explain you are 'practising for a real call'.

Secretly place a whoopee cushion on your chair. Sit on it hard, then burst into tears and plead with the quietest person in the office to stop their campaign of bullying against you.

PUT SOCKS ON YOUR DESK LEGS.
CHANGE THEM DAILY.

SIGN ALL DOCUMENTS WITH A YELLOW WAX
CRAYON.

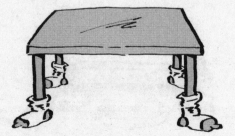

SAY TO YOUR BOSS, 'I LIKE YOUR STYLE' AND SHOOT HIM WITH DOUBLE-BARRELLED FINGERS.

ASK FOR SPONSORSHIP FOR A CHARITY SHAG-A-THON.

Liberally oil your hair and insist that your colleagues call you 'Slick' for the day.

Attach a child's stick-on steering wheel to your monitor, and change your desktop background to a winding road. Pretend to drive.

Prop your monitor on its side and then lie down on your desk as you begin work.

Quietly say, 'You know, talking to yourself is the first sign of madness' to your workmates as you pass their desk.

Use nothing but corporate-speak and buzzwords in all communications for the entire day.

Arrive at work wearing a false neck brace and/or a sling. If a colleague asks what happened, murmur about a bad accident involving a mouse and an ironing board.

Ask to borrow various items of stationery from your colleagues until you have a hoard. Demand payment for their safe return.

Smear ketchup across your nose and then point out to your boss that they have something on their face.

Tell the office you are arranging a birthday bash and everyone is invited, especially if they bring a present. Repeat every week.

Give your colleagues pirate hats and cutlasses, then tell your boss there's a mutiny afoot.

Take advantage of 'dress-down Friday' by wearing a high-visibility vest, fluorescent parachute pants, aviator sunglasses and a fake moustache. Berate your colleagues for not taking the policy seriously.

Ask a colleague on a date and suggest meeting at a strip club.

When delivering post to other departments, wear dark glasses and a false moustache and carry a French newspaper with eyeholes cut into it.

Come back from lunch looking as though you've had a fight (ripped clothing, bloodied nose etc.). When questioned, look shifty and sidle away.

Set a photograph of yourself as your desktop wallpaper. Kiss the screen when everyone is looking.

Take away the coat stand and pretend not to notice, throwing your coat onto the floor where it used to be as you come in.

HOST AN OFFICE PYJAMA PARTY. START A PILLOW FIGHT.

TELL THE ATTENDEES OF A MEETING THAT YOU WILL BE CONDUCTING IT IN SILENCE.

COVER YOUR COMPUTER WITH BUBBLE WRAP.

SEE HOW LOUDLY YOU CAN SHOUT 'BOTTOMS'
WITHOUT BEING FIRED.

Enter an afternoon meeting with your face painted blue and claim to have been abducted by Smurfs during your lunch break.

Claim to have a pet hamster in your desk drawer and attach a water bottle so that it runs upside down into the drawer. Drop sunflower seeds into the drawer every so often.

Eat sweets constantly for a day and discard the wrappers all over the floor.

Burn incense, sprinkle petals on your desk and swap your office chair for cushions and rugs.

To signal the end of a conversation, clamp your hands over your head and go cross-eyed.

Make all decisions for the day with the toss of a coin.

Sit on your chair in the lotus position for twenty minutes. If anyone tries to talk to you, look them in the eye and put your finger to your lips.

Place a banana skin next to your desk and make a show of slipping on it.

BRING A GUITAR TO WORK AND HOLD AN
IMPROMPTU SINGALONG ON YOUR TEA BREAK.

BRING A TOY BABY TO WORK AND CHANGE ITS
NAPPY ON THE DESK.

CULTIVATE A NEW ACCENT I.E. LIVERPUDLIAN, COCKNEY, GERMAN.

ATTACH A SIGN THAT SAYS 'FAX' TO THE PAPER SHREDDER.

Carefully cover your colleague's computer screen with black paper. When they have 'problems' turning it on, tell them that yours has been giving you trouble too. (Extra point if they call an IT technician.)

While using the lift, gasp dramatically every time the doors open.

Tamper with the AutoCorrect feature on a colleague's computer. Replace their name with 'Chump'.

At the end of a meeting, suggest that for once it would be nice if you concluded with a prayer.

Suggest to your boss that they hire less attractive cleaners because you find them a distraction.

At a meeting, arrange toy figures on the table to represent each attendee, move them according to the movements of their real-life counterparts.

Book a male stripper for the office on Friday afternoon.

Place a paperclip on the photocopier and make a few copies, then load these back into the paper tray. The next person to use the copier will be haunted by the 'phantom paperclip'.

3 POINT DARES

Secretly coat the tips of all your pens and pencils in clear nail varnish, which will cause them not to work. Claim it is 'divine intervention' and do nothing for the rest of the day. (The pens can be fixed using nail varnish remover.)

Make your colleagues paperclip jewellery; cry hysterically when they remove it.

Helpfully rearrange everyone's desks into alphabetical order i.e. in tray, keyboard, mug, telephone...

When a member of staff passes by, yell and push them to one side. Say you saved their life and they *owe* you.

Keep a bottle under your desk wrapped in a brown paper bag. Sip it conspicuously throughout the day.

Leap up and scream 'PHONE!' every time the phone rings.

Pick up your bin. Calmly walk over to a colleague's desk and empty all of your rubbish into their bin. Bow politely, and go back to your desk.

Enthusiastically organise an office 'Mexican wave'. Try to introduce another wave... and another... and another... and another... and another...

Find out what your porn star name is (first name = first family pet, surname = street you grew up in) and use it to sign all correspondence.

Begin every sentence with the phrase, 'Back in 'Nam...'

Set up a stationery orchestra to serenade staff members, using various items of office equipment for different instruments.

Mark the next full moon prominently on the office calendar. When it arrives, suddenly leap up howling and run from the office.

Dive under your desk every time you hear a police siren. Climb out sheepishly when it passes and fades away.

Leave notes on a colleague's desk threatening to 'pop a cap in their ass'. Sign it with your graffiti tag.

Bring a slinky into the office and let it fall off your desk. Stare at it for a while, then turn to your nearest colleague and say, 'I think it's broken.'

Invent your own office slang but don't tell anyone else what each word means. Use it constantly and sigh in frustration when others don't understand or become confused.

SWALLOW SACHETS OF DRIED MILK AT REGULAR INTERVALS.

SUDDENLY BECOME INSANELY UPBEAT.
PEPPER YOUR CONVERSATION WITH
WORDS SUCH AS 'MARVELLOUS',
'HUNKY-DORY' AND 'SPIFFING'.

Staple together in pairs any pieces of paper that are placed on your desk for the day, regardless of their irrelevance to one another.

Tell one of your colleagues you had a dream about them last night and would like to explain it to them later. Hint at the sordidness of the dream. Wink at them every time you see them.

In all your documents, underline every word that begins with the first letter of your name.

Sharpen your pencil down to a stub (i.e. less than 1 cm) and complain that you can't do any work due to the 'poor state of the office stationery.'

Tell the quietest person in the office that Thursdays have been made 'wear your partner's clothes to work' day.

Applaud uproariously whenever someone comes out of the toilet.

Whilst eating your lunch, grunt noisily like a pig and lick your lips, then blame it on a blocked nasal passage.

Wrap a co-worker's chair in a bin bag and leave a sign notifying it as 'Under Investigation by the Public Health Authority'.

5 POINT DARES

Peel and slice an onion and try to pass the tears off as mourning for the death of your favourite stick insect.

Say 'meow' instead of 'now' at every available opportunity.

Make your voice boom and talk in an old-fashioned posh accent.

Wait until a moment when everybody in the office is quietly working. Suddenly stand up and scream, 'My God, I've gone deaf!'

COLLAPSE IN THE MIDDLE OF YOUR OFFICE. REPEAT UNTIL YOU HAVE CONVINCED A COLLEAGUE THAT THERE REALLY IS A POLTERGEIST PUSHING YOU OVER.

Groan out loud in a toilet cubicle as if you're in pain.

Wear a tin foil hat and tell anyone who asks that it's to stop the government from reading your thoughts.

Send your colleagues free samples of incontinence pads and say, 'Well, it can't just be me, right?'

Walk like an Egyptian for a day.

Cover your arms with fake tattoos and perch on the corner of your desk, while smoking a pipe and talking about your time at sea.

Interrupt a meeting and tell everyone you have to go and call your probation officer.

When answering the phone, impersonate an old-fashioned sounding policeman e.g. "Ello 'ello 'ello, what's all this then?'

Wear your clothes inside out for a day.

ARRIVE LATE TO A MEETING AND MOONWALK TO YOUR SEAT.

IMITATE A COLLEAGUE AND REPEAT EVERYTHING THEY SAY AND DO.

Bring in a recording of fingernails being scraped across a blackboard. Play throughout the day.

Go for a run before work and insist on walking around the office barefoot to dry off.

Announce juggling to be your new hobby. Practise throughout the day in frantic ten-minute sessions.

Wear 3D glasses to work; if asked, explain with a straight face that they help you to 'see every angle' of your work.

Grin and lick your lips whenever someone approaches your desk.

Prise all the keys from a colleague's keyboard and replace them in the wrong positions. Try to make as many rude words as you can.

Take minutes at meetings using an oversized novelty pencil.

During a meeting, clasp your hands over your head and open your mouth as wide as you can whenever someone suggests an idea of any kind.

SEND A PERSONAL VALENTINE'S EMAIL TO EVERY MEMBER OF STAFF.

ADDRESS EVERYONE IN A MEETING AS 'BORIS', REGARDLESS OF THEIR GENDER.

REPLY TO QUESTIONS WITH THE PHRASE, 'YOU'LL HAVE TO SPEAK TO MY AGENT.'

REMAIN OBLIVIOUS TO THE FACT THAT YOU'VE WORN YOUR PANTS OVER YOUR TROUSERS FOR THE WHOLE DAY.

Fax a black piece of paper to all the office fax machines as many times as you can. When questioned, explain that you were 'seeing how much ink was left in the machines.'

Shout 'bombs away!' every time you send an email with an attachment.

During a meeting, burst through the door dressed as Adam Ant and shout 'Stand and deliver!' whilst wielding two staple guns. Shoot anyone who dares to resist.

Cut a large photo of your boss into a heart shape and ask them to sign it. Flutter your eyelashes accordingly, especially if you're a man.

Write all emails in a comedy Scottish accent. For instance, 'Ach, I dinnae noo where ye wee report hae ended up tae.'

Play a selection of drum 'n' bass tracks as loud as possible during your tea break in the staff room.

Bring six sets of clothes with you to work. Excuse yourself at regular intervals for a 'costume change'.

Buy a box of chocolates and eat its contents in front of your colleagues. Offer them a chocolate after you have eaten the last one, preferably with your mouth full.

Fill the kitchen sink with custard.

Provide a running commentary during a meeting, highlighting who is looking bored, who is talking too much and who is looking the least comfortable in their seat. Offer a 'post-meeting analysis' when people leave the conference room.

Put your chair and desk in the lift and work there for a day.

Men – wear a flowery dress and heels to the office and ask to be called 'Sally'.

Women – paint a moustache on your face, wear a pinstripe suit and ask to be known as 'Bruce'.

Put a call through to your boss, telling him it's a Mr O. Bin Laden.

Consume fibrous and gassy food and drink for a whole week. Enjoy the effect on your workmates.

Insist on Eskimo-kissing everyone you come into contact with throughout the day.

Learn the first movement of one of Wagner's operas and sing it at the top of your voice in the middle of the office.

Commandeer the waste-paper basket and tell everyone they can only throw something away if they slam-dunk it and shout 'Basket!'

Bring in a skateboard and use it to get around the office, deliberately knocking things off people's desks and crashing into colleagues.

Talk like Dick Van Dyke in *Mary Poppins* for a week.

Insist on shouting whilst using the phone, increasing in volume the further away the person is on the other end.

Spread a rumour that a previously unpopular colleague has won the lottery, and laugh as everyone tries to befriend them.

Sneak into the office early and spread imitation snow everywhere. Claim you can't get into work due to adverse weather.

Order a massive bouquet of flowers to be delivered to your desk, with a note from the US president thanking you for saving his life.

SHAVE YOUR ARMPITS IN THE MIDDLE OF THE
OFFICE.

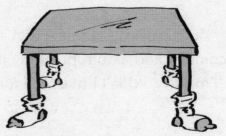

PULL OUT ALL THE PLUGS IN THE OFFICE AND
CLAIM THE 'POWER GREMLINS'
HAVE STRUCK AGAIN.

Wait until a very quiet moment and scream 'Duck!'

Put decaf in the coffee maker for three weeks. Once everyone has got over their caffeine addictions, switch to espresso.

Put mosquito netting around your work space and play a recording of tropical sounds all day.

Ask a colleague to explain something very complicated. Interrupt them midway by saying, 'I'm sorry, I don't have time for this. Some of us have got work to do.'

Leave a note marked 'URGENT' on a colleague's desk saying, 'I need those figures by lunchtime. This deadline CANNOT be extended.' Leave no contact details.

Decorate your work space with photos of the Krankies. Try to pass them off as your children.

Cover the lenses of your glasses with pictures of eyes cut out of magazines. Put them on every time your boss passes your desk.

Wear an unusual sporting uniform to work e.g. cricket whites, scuba mask, boxing gloves. Tell people you are 'in training'.

Give yourself a full manicure at your desk. Then give yourself a full pedicure.

Fashion a long poking device from office stationery. Use it to stroke your colleague's face while they are on the phone.

Instead of taking notes in a meeting, draw an abstract sketch of your boss. Leave it on the table as you leave.

Five days in advance of your next meeting, call each of your colleagues to tell them you are unable to attend as you are not in the mood.

Sit at your desk and type nothing but 'All work and no play makes Jack a dull boy.' If anyone questions you, sternly tell them you are working on an important piece of work and are too busy to be disturbed.

Bring along a hand puppet to a meeting. Ask it to clarify difficult points.

Present each of your colleagues with a cup of coffee and a biscuit. Smash each biscuit with your fist.

During a meeting, excuse yourself to go to the bathroom. Come back with the entire front of your trousers wet.

Speed up your boss's mouse so it is uncontrollable. Advise them to cut back on the caffeine.

Replace a colleague's mouse with some cheese and a note saying, 'If you don't pay up, your mouse gets it.'

Ignore the first five people who say good morning to you. Kiss the sixth.

Arrange a staff night out. Make sure your boss is told to arrive twenty minutes before anyone else.

NO MATTER WHAT ANYONE ASKS YOU, REPLY 'OK'. KEEP THIS UP FOR A WHOLE DAY.

ANNOUNCE WHEN YOU ARE GOING TO THE BATHROOM. BE SURE TO SPECIFY WHICH NUMBER IT WILL BE.

SET UP A NEW OUT OF OFFICE AUTO-REPLY
MESSAGE ON YOUR EMAIL BEFORE YOUR NEXT DAY
OFF. SOME SUGGESTIONS:

A) I WILL BE OUT OF THE OFFICE FOR TWO WEEKS
FOR MEDICAL REASONS. WHEN I RETURN, PLEASE
REFER TO ME AS BEV INSTEAD OF DAVE.

B) I AM OUT OF THE OFFICE TODAY. PLEASE BE
PATIENT AND YOUR EMAILS WILL BE DELETED IN
THE ORDER IN WHICH THEY WERE RECEIVED.

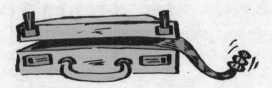

As everyone leaves the office for the day, thank them for coming and give them a goody bag.

Arrive at work wearing combats and a balaclava. When questioned, reply, 'I'm afraid I can't talk about it.'

Arrange for a barbershop quartet to arrive in your boss's office at 9 a.m. on Monday, singing the national anthem.

On arrival in the morning, kiss everyone in the office on both cheeks. Whisper compliments to the men between kisses, like 'Mmmm, you smell so good!'

OUTRAGEOUS OFFICE DARES

Offer to arrange the office Christmas party. Say you will be holding it at KFC and charge everyone £10 each.

If someone offers to make you a cup of tea, break into uncontrollable sobs and exclaim, 'That is the nicest thing anyone has ever said to me.' Ask for a hug.

Walk into a very busy person's office and, while they watch you with growing irritation, turn the light switch off and on ten times.

When a colleague of the opposite sex comes to talk to you, hold up your hand and say, 'Look, I know what you're going to ask me... For the last time, NO, I will not practise tonsil hockey with you!'

5 POINT DARES

Ask your boss how long it will be until a computer takes over their job.

Perform stretches around the office throughout the day. Be sure to invade everyone's personal space. Start by placing one foot on your neighbour's desk and grunting.

Leave a note on a colleague's desk saying a 'Mr Lyon' phoned or a 'Mr Griller'. Then list the number of the local zoo.

Run a lap of the office at high speed. Look at your watch and announce a personal best. Repeat until physically restrained.

Appoint yourself 'Head of Office Safety'. Kindly upholster colleagues in bubble wrap.

Buy some miniature farm animals and turn your desk into a pastoral scene. Bellow softly throughout the day.

Paint the office walls black overnight. In the morning, tell everyone eternal darkness has come and they will all have to go home.

Create a mini aquarium in the water cooler. Add a rubber duck, fake weed, fluorescent pirate ships...

CUT A SQUARE HOLE IN A CARDBOARD BOX, DRAW ON BUTTONS AND KNOBS AND PUT IT ON YOUR HEAD. GIVE LIVE 'NEWS REPORTS' OF YOUR CO-WORKERS' BANAL ACTIVITIES, COMPLETE WITH YOUR OWN FAST-PACED THEME TUNE.

Ask your boss, 'If a deranged gun-toting maniac came in and tried to shoot me, would you take the bullet?'

Turn around and stare longingly at a colleague every few minutes. Mouth the words 'Call me'.

Methodically wink at each staff member during an important presentation.

Write onto your boss's calendar: 'SHOPPING FOR A NEW HANDBAG FOR THE DRAG QUEEN CONVENTION'. When he gets angry, give him a knowing smile and say, 'It's a devil to find one in pink PVC, isn't it?'

Move around the office as if trapped inside a computer game. Stealth along the walls, cock your fake gun and include suitably elaborate sound effects.

Go into the finance department and wait until someone looks as if they are deep in calculation. Begin shouting random numbers at them with increasing volume and frequency.

Make a life-sized model of yourself and sit it at your desk, then leave the office, explaining to your colleagues that your twin will be taking your place for the day.

Ask your colleagues for the loan of obscenely large amounts of money (at least £5,000) and refuse to speak to them unless they agree to the loan.

ASK FOR TWENTY MINUTES MATERNITY LEAVE IN THE DAY TO HAVE A BABY, EXPLAINING THAT BIRTHING PROCEDURES HAVE RECENTLY IMPROVED DRAMATICALLY.

MOVE AROUND THE OFFICE BY 'SWIMMING' ALONG THE FLOOR.

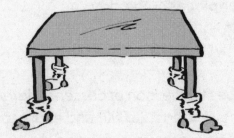

Bring your pillow and duvet to work and go to sleep on your desk, claiming you are most productive when well rested.

Bring in a fishing rod and waders and fish from your desk on your breaks.

Sign all your correspondence with the catchphrase and initials of your favourite film character e.g. 'Out for lunch until one. I'll be back. A. S.'

Make a full English breakfast in the morning before work and pack it into a lunch box, then eat it cold in front of your colleagues at lunch time.

Tie a ball and chain to your ankle and refer to your colleagues as 'fellow inmates' in front of your boss.

Use irritatingly empty clichés in response to every question e.g. 'Never judge a book by its cover' and 'Your guess is as good as mine.'

Send an email asking everyone to observe a ten-minute silence in respect for your childhood pet that died when you were six.

Find out how to insult your boss in Swahili and do it at every opportunity.

Suddenly stand up from your desk, gasp and wrestle yourself violently to the floor.

In the middle of a meeting, stand up and demand to know the real reason the meeting has been called.

Take a register before beginning a meeting, insisting on being called Sir/Miss.

Install cardboard CCTV cameras around the office and inform everyone that you are watching their every move.

Fashion a 'volume control' switch from cardboard. Carry it around and use it to adjust the volume of your voice when you speak to your colleagues.

Wear enormous comedy glasses to work, explaining that you went for an eye test and the optician said you were short-sighted.

Carry a magnifying glass and use it to examine documents from your colleagues for suspect stains and marks.

Remove all the files from a colleague's filing cabinet and fill it with colourful helium balloons.

10 POINT DARES

Hide a kitten in a filing cabinet.

Come into work looking dazed and claim to have seen aliens in your back garden the previous night. Try to convince at least three people you genuinely believe it.

Blow up condoms and tie them up around the office with banners celebrating the relationship between your boss and his secretary.

Remove all chairs but one from the meeting room. Insist that everyone sit on the floor whilst sitting firmly in your seat.

SCRATCH YOUR GROIN AND COMPLAIN ABOUT A 'YEAST INFECTION'.

AT THE END OF A MEETING, 'FIRE' YOUR BOSS IN THE STYLE OF SIR ALAN SUGAR.

Wear shiny black PVC and tell everyone it's a lifestyle choice. Whip optional.

Wear tap shoes to a meeting. At a quiet moment, jump up and give an impromptu dance for the pleasure of the attendees.

Serenade your boss at the Christmas party with 'All I Want for Christmas Is You'. (Extra point if their partner is present.)

Chair an important shareholder's meeting in total darkness. Hold a torch under your chin as you explain in a spooky voice that the prices of your company's shares are dropping at a 'scary' rate.

At the end of a meeting, drop a pen. When someone bends down to pick it up, scream 'That's mine!' and run away. Later in the day, email them asking them not to touch your belongings in future.

Give an anonymous tip-off to the police, suggesting they raid the office for drugs and stolen jewellery.

Add a small 'B' to the lettering on your boss's 'in tray'. Point this out to your boss after you've poured all your rubbish onto their incoming documents.

Nail your sleeve to your boss's desk while they are on lunch and try to appear nonchalant upon their return.

Spend the whole morning eating marshmallows until you are sick, then take the afternoon off claiming you 'have a virus'.

Write a letter to head office explaining that your boss is rubbish and apply for his/her job, then sign it from a colleague.

Smoke a large, suspicious roll-up at your desk, explaining that you 'need to get into the mood for the Bob Marley concert this evening.' Act distraught when someone points out that Bob Marley is dead.

Steal your boss's computer and leave a note in its place reading: IOU 1 x Comp. xxx.

Secrete an alarm and gas mask into the office. Set off the alarm, quickly put on the gas mask and usher everyone outside, shouting, 'Gas! Gas!'

Use coats as posts and play full contact rugby in the office.

Forward all spam email involving Viagra or weight loss to your boss, saying, 'I thought you might find this of interest.'

Release pigeons into the office ventilation ducts.

DRAW A CRUDE TATTOO ON YOUR BUTTOCKS WITH MARKER PEN AND SHOW EVERYONE IN THE OFFICE, TELLING THEM IT'S REAL AND CLAIMING YOU HAD IT DONE AS A BET WHILE DRUNK.

INVITE YOUR BOSS FOR A DRINK AFTER WORK TO DISCUSS A MASSIVE PAY RISE.

10 POINT DARES

Send out notes on your boss's personalised paper threatening to fire people unless they now follow *your* orders.

Invite the office intern to your 'wedding', and give them a location. Hide there and watch as they turn up looking confused.

Phone your own office pretending to be an angry customer. Threaten to burn down the office. Then hang up and set off the fire alarm.

Bring a zoo animal into the office:
snake – 5 points
bear – 10 points
hippo – 15 points
red-plumed cassowary – 30 points

Whilst giving an important presentation replace a simple, frequently-used word, such as 'the', with 'bollocks'.

Arrive late to a meeting, apologise and claim that you didn't have time for lunch so you will be nibbling during the session. Eat an entire raw potato.

Walk into your boss's office and have this conversation:
'Can you hear that?'
'What?'
'Never mind, it's gone now.'
Repeat at regular intervals throughout the day.

Switch the contents of all the bottles of Coke with vinegar in the office kitchen.

YODEL INSTEAD OF SPEAKING FOR THE DAY.

GO UP TO A YOUNGER MEMBER OF THE OFFICE,
SIT ON THEIR LAP AND SHOUT OUT TO THE REST
OF THE OFFICE, 'YOU'VE BEEN A BAD,
BAD BABYSITTER!'

Try to squash yourself into a filing cabinet drawer. When questioned, claim to have seen a leprechaun climb in and explain that you were trying to follow him to ask for some gold.

Ask if anyone would like an ice cream, then return to the office hours later with them all melted.

Communicate with everyone through the medium of dance for the day.

Walk with a strange limp and don't sit down for the day, claiming to have had a horrible but unspecified accident with a banana.

Phone your boss's spouse and tearfully confess to an affair. (Extra point if you pretend to be another member of staff.)

Sign your boss up for a year's subscription to a top-shelf magazine.

Burst into floods of tears for exactly three minutes, then stop and carry on with what you were doing. Repeat hourly.

Take a phone call and plead loudly with the caller not to do anything silly. Tell them you will meet their demands and ask for the release of the prime minister. Then hang up and continue working as though nothing has happened.

GIVE YOURSELF A FACE MASK
TREATMENT DURING A TEA BREAK;
PUT CUCUMBER SLICES ON YOUR
EYES AND APPLY LIBERAL AMOUNTS
OF MUD TO YOUR FACE AND NECK.
(EXTRA POINT IF YOU WEAR A
DRESSING GOWN AND DISPOSABLE
PANTS.)

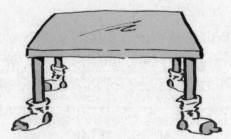

Email your colleagues saying you need to take sick leave as you've caught a computer virus. Suggest they take the proper precautions.

Buy your boss a can of deodorant and suggest they use it. (Extra point if you have a clothes peg on your nose while handing it to them.)

Buy a fish from the fishmongers and hide it somewhere in the office. Try to leave it there for at least a month.

Dust your desk for fingerprints and look suspiciously at your nearest colleagues. Seal everything on your desk into 'evidence bags' and take it away in a sack. Use duct tape to make a cordon around your desk.

COLOUR YOUR FACE WITH A YELLOW HIGHLIGHTER PEN AND SAY YOU'VE GOT JAUNDICE.

WRITE AN ELABORATE RESIGNATION LETTER, DETAILING YOUR BOSS'S SHORTCOMINGS AND INADEQUACIES. ADD A PTO NOTE – 'ONLY KIDDING!'

THE GRAND TOTAL

There were a total of approximately 1,500 points to be awarded.

If you scored 0–500 points:

You're a loser – simple as that. You deserve every moment of office boredom coming to you.

If you scored 500–1,000 points:

Well you certainly tried didn't you? You deserve a medal for all the stupid things you have done and for all the confusion you have inflicted upon your colleagues.

If you scored 1,000+ points:

You are the ultimate daredevil, on a par with Evel Knievel. You are officially king or queen of the office.

Have you enjoyed this book? If so, why not write a
review on your favourite website?

Thanks very much for buying this Summersdale book.

www.summersdale.com